Everything You Need to Know About

RACISM

Understanding racism begins by examining our own attitudes and prejudices toward others.

• THE NEED TO KNOW LIBRARY •

Everything You Need to Know About

RACISM

Nasoan Sheftel-Gomes

THE ROSEN PUBLISHING GROUP, INC.
NEW YORK

To my grandparents, for their love. To my parents, for teaching me to be open-minded and for supporting me in everything I do. To Aumijo, for listening.

Special thanks go to Cassius Gil's 9th- and 10th-grade classes at Fannie Lou Hamer Freedom High School, Bronx, NY, Alex Milton's 7th grade class at The Little Red School House in New York City, and students from the Multicultural Student Conference Planning Committee at the Diversity Resource Collaborative. Thank you for "telling it like it is!"

Published in 1998 by The Rosen Publishing Group, Inc.
29 East 21st Street, New York, NY 10010

First Edition
Copyright © 1998 by The Rosen Publishing Group, Inc.

Library of Congress Cataloging-in-Publication Data

Sheftel-Gomes, Nasoan.
    Everything you need to know about racism / Nasoan Sheftel-Gomes. - 1st ed.
        p. cm.
    Includes bibliographical references and index.
    Summary: Discusses the nature and effects of racism and ways to deal with it and take a stand against it.
    ISBN: 0-8239-2057-7
    1. Racism—United States—Juvenile literature. 2. Social conflict—United States—Juvenile literature. 3. United States—Race relations—Juvenile literature. [1. Racism. 2. Race relations. 3. Prejudice.] I. Title.
E184.A1S574 1998
305.8'00973—dc2
                                                    98-11390
                                                         CIP
                                                          AC

Manufactured in the United States of America.

Contents

Introduction

*M*aria is a sixteen-year-old, first-generation Mexican American who, like many teenagers, enjoys spending Saturdays at the mall. She usually meets up with five or six of her girlfriends to shop, eat, and check out some of the cute guys who hang out there. Lately, however, Maria has begun to notice that when she browses in some of the stores, the salespeople follow her around. She feels singled out because the salespeople don't do this to her friends, who are white. Maria feels uncomfortable saying anything to her friends because she doesn't think that they will understand her. She's afraid they may say she is overreacting or imagining things. So instead, Maria has stopped going to the mall altogether, and when her friends ask her why she won't go out with them, she just tells them she has things to do at home.

Opposing reactions to the verdict of O. J. Simpson's criminal trial made race issues the subject of debate across the country.

What is racism? Will I know it when I see it? What can I do about it when it confronts me? When people think of racism they often think of name-calling, but racism involves much more than verbal insults. Racism comes in many different forms. It can be as obvious as name-calling or as subtle as making assumptions about someone based on race. Sometimes racism is hard to prove. We may feel we are being discriminated against, but we can't be sure. It's not always easy to understand another person's motivations. This makes racism even more complicated.

You may already have seen many images of racial conflict in the news. These images include Rodney King being beaten on a Los Angeles freeway by white police

officers and the L.A. riots that followed the trial when
the white officers were acquitted. Many will never forget how the country was split racially in their reactions
to the O. J. Simpson verdict. You may also have seen
films from the civil rights movement of the 1960s show-
ing peaceful protesters being attacked by policemen in
riot gear with fire hoses and attack dogs.

These are a few of the more extreme examples of
racial prejudice and hatred in the United States, but they
are not the most common ones. As in Maria's case,
racism can be subtle and hard to pin down. You may
feel its effects and still be unable to explain it to others.

At one time in our history, racism was very easy to
see. Black Americans had fewer rights and fewer opportunities than white Americans. Blacks were not allowed
to vote, own property, or live wherever they wanted.
They could not attend the schools of their choice. In the
past, these freedoms were kept from blacks by segregation laws. Black Americans faced a constant threat of
violence and punishment if they did not follow those
laws. The civil rights movement changed those laws and
helped blacks and all minorities achieve equal rights.

Today there are other laws in place that are meant to
prevent the most harmful and obvious forms of racism.
Now blacks and other ethnic groups have the right to
vote, live wherever they want, and attend any school,
because of these laws. But even with these laws against
discrimination, many subtle, as well as violent, displays
of racism still exist.

All ethnic groups, from Mexican American to Native American to African American to Asian American and many more, have experienced the painful reality of being viewed and treated as "the other" or "the outsider" in our society. As a result, these peoples are linked by a history of struggle to belong. Unfortunately, they often don't feel linked. Many times ethnic groups can discriminate against one another as well.

One of the keys to eliminating racism is to change ignorant attitudes that you or someone you know may have. Unfortunately, many people have racist attitudes even if they may not want to admit it. It's important for people to be honest with themselves about their own prejudices and for them to recognize racism in all of its forms—from the obvious to the hidden. Learning about other people's cultures and traditions is also necessary for there to be acceptance and respect between different ethnic groups.

Lastly, we must recognize that our future is dependent on how we treat each other as individuals. Frederick Douglass, former slave, abolitionist, and author, once said, "The destiny of the colored American. . .is the destiny of America." Whether we are black or white or of any other race, we are all Americans, and as Americans, we are dependent on one another to move forward as a nation. As part of the next generation, you can help make a difference in the fight against racism.

Explorer Christopher Columbus is often given credit for discovering America, even though it was already inhabited by native peoples.

Chapter 1

A Brief History of Racism in the United States

Racism is the belief that one race of people is better than all others. It's the idea that human worth and ability are based on your race. Racism is also the hostility that some people feel for each other because of their different races. By understanding the roots of racism, you will be better able to understand how racism affects you—whatever your race may be.

"Discovering" America

In August 1492, the explorer Christopher Columbus set sail with three ships toward what he thought was Asia in search of the "riches of the Orient." Instead, Columbus "discovered" America on October 12, 1492, when he caught sight of the Bahamas. The natives, the Arawak Indians, swam from shore to greet him. Columbus took these native peoples aboard his ship as slaves and insisted they show him where to find the gold he had promised the king and queen of Spain, who had sponsored the trip.

In 1494, on a second trip, Columbus again traveled to the Caribbean in search of gold. After finding none, Columbus and his men imprisoned more than 11,000 Arawak men, women, and children; they even tried to take 500 of them back to Spain. Two hundred died on the hard journey, while those who remained in their homeland were forced to search for gold. If they didn't find any they were tortured—their hands were cut off and they were left to bleed to death. In two years, half of the 250,000 Indians on what is now Haiti were dead.

Slave Labor

By the early 1800s, nearly 4 million black slaves lived and worked in the United States. Many of them were shipped to the United States after being stolen or sold in their native Africa. Those who survived the dangerous trip by boat to America were sold or auctioned off to white plantation owners, who used the Africans to work their fields, serve their families, and clean their houses.

The African slaves were treated as badly as and sometimes worse than the farmers' animals. They were beaten, whipped, tortured, and made to work long hours in the fields for no pay. Slaveowners could do what they pleased with their slaves—even kill them—and it was not against the law. Slaveowners destroyed families by

Slaveowners bought and sold Africans, forcing them into a life of slavery.

separating mothers from their children and husbands from their wives. Many slaves attempted to run away and find their family members, but this was punishable by harsh laws.

In 1850 the Fugitive Slave Act was passed. The act made it easy for slaveowners to recapture former slaves or simply to pick up blacks they said had escaped. During that time, one thousand slaves a year had escaped to the North, where blacks were free from slavery, but not necessarily free from racism. Many of the slaves who made it north had the help of free blacks who risked their lives to help them escape, as well as northern white abolitionists who didn't believe in slavery.

Slavery was a main issue surrounding the Civil War and was abolished when the war ended.

The Underground Railroad

Harriet Tubman was born into slavery. She managed to escape and went on to become the most famous conductor on the Underground Railroad. The Underground Railroad was a network of houses and other places organized by free blacks and sympathetic whites to help black slaves escape. The Underground Railroad helped thousands of slaves to freedom. Harriet Tubman herself made 199 dangerous trips back and forth, and overall she helped more than three hundred slaves to freedom.

During this period, the U. S. economy and land holdings continued to expand. This growth was achieved by the use of black slave labor and the purchases of land from European countries. Furthermore, white pioneers moved farther west, claiming land as they went. Native Americans were considered obstacles in the path of westward expansion. They were forced off their land and either went west or fought, and most often died, for their land.

The Civil War (1861–1865)

In 1861, the Civil War began after the election of President Abraham Lincoln, who opposed the spread of slavery. Eleven southern states (the Confederacy) seceded, or separated, from the North (the Union). Southerners believed that President Lincoln was out to change their way of life, including slavery, and they fought the northern states who supported his presidency. Slavery was a central issue in the Civil War. The Confederacy wanted to maintain slavery while the Union wanted to abolish it.

In an attempt to get the southern states to reenter the Union, President Lincoln issued the Emancipation Proclamation on January 1, 1863. It was meant to punish the southern states that continued to fight against the Union. In hopes of preserving the Union, the Proclamation said that slaves in those southern states that continued to fight against the North were free. But the Proclamation did not free the slaves who lived in states that remained a part of the Union.

Reconstruction (1865–1877)

When slavery was abolished in 1865, blacks enjoyed a

After Reconstruction, southern states enacted segregation laws. Blacks were forced to use separate, often inferior, facilities, such as schools, hospitals, restaurants, and restrooms.

temporary improvement in their quality of life during the post-Civil War period called Reconstruction. But many were still poor and uneducated. Reconstruction was a period of about twenty years when blacks were able to vote, hold political office, and start schools. It was a period of hope. During Reconstruction, blacks were divided about what rights to pursue now that they were free. Blacks had more opportunities than ever before, but some whites were becoming nervous about sharing their power.

In 1877, Reconstruction ended and violence and terror erupted in the South. Beatings, murders, and race riots became common, and many blacks were killed. Much of the violence came from the Ku Klux Klan (KKK), a terrorist group in the South that formed in 1866 and whose members believed in white supremacy. Men in the KKK wore white sheets and burned crosses in the yards of black people's homes. Many blacks were lynched by the angry mobs of hooded men who attacked with no warning. These attacks were used to keep blacks from voting through fear and intimidation.

Segregation Laws

In the twentieth century, more and more black people moved to the North in search of better jobs and better lives. However, even in the northern cities segregation existed in housing and schools. In the 1896 Supreme Court case called *Plessy vs. Ferguson*, the court ruled that having separate but equal schools, transportation, and housing for blacks and whites was legal. Therefore, segregation was legal.

In the South, Jim Crow laws were developed to make sure blacks and whites lived separately. These laws kept blacks and whites segregated from one another as much as possible and kept blacks poor and without power. They were forced to use separate water fountains labeled "colored," and they were forced to sit at the back of the bus and to give up their seats if a white person was standing. They were not allowed in some places at all. Black schools were not as good as white schools, and living conditions for blacks were bad. What blacks had was separate, but it was not equal.

From 1820 to 1930, 60 percent of the world's immigrants came to the United States. Many came through Ellis Island outside of New York City, pictured here.

Immigrants

Racism didn't affect only blacks and Native Americans. During this time immigrants were pouring into the United States from all over Europe. They were mostly poor, and many were without anything when they arrived. Some, like the Jewish immigrants, were fleeing persecution in their own countries. The huge numbers of immigrants who were looking for work kept wages very low (because they would work for little pay) and, as a result, many Americans suffered under poor working conditions.

Even though the United States is a country made up of immigrants, the new immigrants were looked down upon in their new home. Racism existed even between immigrant groups because there was so much competition for the few opportunities that were available. For example, many Irish immigrants who had been in America for a while resented the new Jewish immigrants moving into their neighborhoods. In one incident in 1902 in New York, a large Jewish funeral for an important rabbi was attacked by an angry mob of Irish people. The police force was mostly Irish at that time, and an official investigation proved that Irish policemen helped the rioters.

By 1880 there were 75,000 Chinese immigrants in California. They had been brought in by the railroad companies to do the difficult work of building railroads. The Chinese immigrants were segregated from whites in schools and were not allowed to vote. They were subjected to continual violence. Many laws were created to

keep the Chinese from having equal opportunities. The
Chinese Exclusion Act of 1882 prohibited more Chinese
laborers from even entering the country.

The roots of racism run deep in the United States.
Many people fought hard to change the laws and the attitudes that helped build this country. Fighting racism has
always been a difficult struggle. And the struggle continues today. The next chapter discusses some of the
important events and people of the civil rights movement.

Chapter 2

The Civil Rights Movement

The National Association for the Advancement of Colored People (NAACP) was founded in 1909. It fought many civil rights battles. The NAACP's most notable victory was the landmark decision of the Supreme Court in *Brown vs. Board of Education*.

On May 17, 1954, the Supreme Court ruled unanimously that segregated schools were unconstitutional. On September 5, 1957, nine black students reported for school at Central High School in Little Rock, Arkansas, as the entire nation watched. Those students became known as the "Little Rock Nine." Because of the invention of television, Americans were able to see the fight that some white Arkansans waged to keep their schools all white.

The nine students were met by an angry mob of whites who were determined to keep their schools

Rosa Parks's refusal to give up her seat on a public bus sparked the Montgomery bus boycott, which ended segregation on public transportation.

separate. The white protesters screamed ugly names. The students were turned away at the door of the school. Two weeks later, U.S. president Dwight Eisenhower sent in federal troops to escort the black students into the school. The students had finally succeeded in getting an equal education. Meanwhile, the civil rights movement was taking shape, and distinctive leaders were emerging.

Rosa Parks

On December 1, 1955, Rosa Parks got on a bus to go home. When a white passenger got on the bus, the bus driver ordered her to give up her seat, but Mrs. Parks refused to move. She was arrested and thrown in jail.

The black people of Montgomery, Alabama, decided to do something about the law. Mrs. Parks filed a lawsuit, and the black people of Montgomery boycotted the buses. Dr. Martin Luther King, Jr., a young minister at the local church, became the leader of the Montgomery bus boycott.

After thirteen months, the laws were finally changed, and blacks were given the right to sit wherever they wanted on the bus—first come, first served. It was another major victory in the fight for equal rights.

Dr. Martin Luther King, Jr.

Dr. Martin Luther King, Jr., later became a great leader in the civil rights movement. He was known for his belief in peaceful protest, and he helped black

Americans make strides toward equality before he was assassinated in 1968. Dr. King's strategy of nonviolent protest won him the support of many Northerners, both black and white. In 1963, he organized the March on Washington. He delivered his "I Have a Dream" speech to more than 200,000 people. Because of his work, President John F. Kennedy supported a ban on discrimination. Many of the antidiscrimination laws passed, such as the Voting Rights Act of 1965, came into effect during President Lyndon Johnson's term.

Malcolm X

The black-power movement had its heyday in the late 1960s and early 1970s. It was started by younger blacks who wanted to have the same opportunities as whites. These young men and women believed that peaceful protests were not getting them far enough. One of the leaders of the black power movement was Malcolm X. He believed that blacks should gain their rights "by any means necessary." He was a Muslim minister when he became a prominent leader. Although he became less militant later in life, he believed that blacks could rely only on themselves for equality. In 1965, Malcolm X was assassinated while making a speech in New York.

Hundreds and thousands of black and white people fought for civil rights in the 1960s. Many Americans were shocked by the images they saw on television of peaceful protesters being hosed by water and attacked

A year before his assassination, Malcolm X converted to Islam and promoted brotherhood between blacks and whites.

by dogs. People like Martin Luther King, Jr., Rosa Parks, and Malcolm X are among the most prominent leaders of the civil rights movement. There were younger, less well-known people who also made a difference, including students whose "sit-ins" at segregated lunch counters allowed people of all races to eat together. Most important, there were those like Emmet Till, a fourteen-year-old black boy from Chicago who was murdered because he spoke to a white woman. His tragic and senseless death helped all Americans see the evils of racism and forced them to do something about it.

By the end of the 1960s, many changes had occurred in the United States. One of these changes was the establishment of the affirmative action policy. It was designed to increase the proportion of minorities in the workplace and in schools long dominated by whites. In general, the policy requires employers and institutions to set goals for hiring or admitting members of minority groups.

Affirmative action has always been controversial. Many opponents call it "reverse discrimination." The 1990s have seen a huge backlash against affirmative action. Some states have voted against it, and it continues to spark debate in universities and in the workplace all over the United States. Race continues to be a complex issue for all Americans, and the struggle to deal with racism affects many people today.

Chapter 3

How Does Racism Affect Me?

In this decade, racism has changed. It is sometimes less obvious, but it can still be hurtful. Many of us wrongly assume that the only racists are members of the Ku Klux Klan, neo-Nazi groups, or white supremacist organizations. But the truth is that not all racists wear signs proclaiming their bigotry. They may not even believe that their attitudes are racist.

The tricky thing about racism today is that because racial prejudice tends to be more subtle, it is also more difficult to recognize and eliminate. Racial prejudice is harder to confront when it's not out in the open. Remember how helpless Maria felt in her situation as described in the introduction of this book? It would have been easier for her to confront the salesperson if he had called her a name or had posted signs saying "whites only."

You will learn about many stereotypes and racial prejudices in this chapter. Stereotypes and lack of knowledge about people's differences can be extremely harmful and contribute to the cycle of racism in our country.

Rob was ecstatic! He had just received a call from a popular magazine asking him to come in for a job interview. He had been looking for weeks and, he thought, this could be the big break in his search for a summer job. On the day of the interview, Rob arrived at the skyscraper office building neatly dressed in a suit and tie. He asked the man behind the desk in the lobby for directions to the magazine's offices. The man looked him over, and then pointed him toward a bank of elevators. Rob thanked him and eagerly went on his way.

But when Rob got there, he found that he had been directed to the service elevators for bike messengers and deliverymen. How had he been mistaken? He was dressed professionally, he spoke politely, and more important he wasn't wearing a bike helmet or uniform. The one thing he did have in common with the bike messengers and deliverymen was that a lot of them were minorities. The truth was that very few professionals in this building were nonwhite. He could feel the frustration welling up inside. Rob didn't want to let the experience shake his confidence, so he shrugged off his anger and asked someone for directions to the elevators for visitors and employees. He was determined to get that job.

The Ku Klux Klan has a long history of violence against blacks and other ethnic groups.

What happened to Rob is an example of how often people are judged by the way they look. In this case, black deliverymen and messengers often came to the office building where Rob was to have his interview. The guard mistakenly assumed that because Rob was black and was in this building, he must be a messenger. The guard didn't bother to see Rob for who he really was: a well-dressed young man with a résumé in his hand on his way to an interview.

Sometimes this sort of misunderstanding may seem harmless. But when it happens to a person over and over again, it can affect that person's self-esteem. This time, Rob was able to let it roll off his back and go to his interview with confidence. But not everyone can

Everyone makes judgments about people based on their appearance. Learning to look past physical qualities can help combat prejudice.

avoid the negativity of stereotyping—whether you're black, white, Hispanic, Asian, or any other race.

For many white people, it can be easy to forget about their race. Often, the only time whites may think about being white is when they find themselves in a room full of people of another race. Even in this situation, a white person may be thinking more about the race of the other people than his or her own. But if you are a person of color, you may be judged or singled out for the color of your skin every time you walk down the street, go to work or school, enter a store, go to a movie, or eat at a restaurant. In addition, when you read a magazine, go to a movie, or watch television, you may often see that your race is unfairly portrayed—or not seen at all.

Stereotypes

Too often it is easier to forget that each person is unique. If people weren't so quick to judge, we wouldn't hear prejudiced statements such as, "Black people are dangerous" or "Mexicans are lazy" or "White people think they know everything." These kinds of statements are based on stereotypes. A stereotype is an unfair assumption formed when the actions of one person become the basis for judging a whole group of people. Stereotypes are usually negative and based on ignorance. If you have never known someone of another race, it might be easy to think you know about them based on statements you have heard others make or something you have seen on television.

The media have a huge influence on people's opinions and attitudes and can indirectly contribute to racism.

The Media

Stereotypes are everywhere, especially in the media. The media include television, movies, newspapers, magazines, radio, and even the Internet. Each medium provides information and entertainment about many different things. The media have the power to influence many people. Unfortunately, the media can also promote negative stereotypes.

When you watch television or go to a movie, you often see characters portrayed in a way that doesn't present a complete or honest picture. For example, if you were to watch a whole week's worth of prime-time television, you might notice that the criminals are usually black, drug dealers are often Hispanic, or white people are often rich. But in reality, there are many white people who aren't rich, and there are criminals of every race.

Sometimes you may not even see a person of color at all. Many of the most popular shows on television do not have any nonwhite characters. The same can be said of magazines. How many pictures show white men and women? As a young black, Hispanic, or Asian male or female, you might feel less attractive or interesting because you don't see your race among these images.

Beauty "Ideals"

Young women who don't look like the so-called "All-American beauty" sometimes try to alter their appearance. Some try things as extreme as bleaching their skin or changing the shape of their eyes, nose, or body with plastic surgery. Within different cultures, there are certain beauty "ideals" that are valued more than others.

Every culture has different beauty standards. For example, in Ethiopian culture women with wide-set eyes and straight, distinct noses are considered beautiful. In other African cultures, women elongate their necks with elaborate neckpieces, and this too is considered beautiful. Ideas of what is beautiful change throughout history, and vary from culture to culture.

Ultimately, beauty has less to do with outward appearances and more to do with inner qualities, such as intelligence and a sense of humor. We can all work on appreciating people for their differences and admiring people not only physically, but also for their unique personalities.

Making Judgments

When people make judgments that aren't true, it can really hurt. It's an easy thing to do. In some ways we all make judgments. The first thing you may see about a person is skin color or style of clothes. Oftentimes we use things like clothing and hairstyles to give us clues about people, such as where they are from or what they may like. If you are used to hanging out with people who are like you, then you may be uncomfortable with someone who looks different.

For many reasons, you and your family may never have been exposed to people of different races, religions, or family traditions. It could be because of where you live, who your parents' friends are, or what kind of school you attend. When you have no exposure to different types of people, it can be easy to stereotype. The best way to avoid stereotyping is to be aware and try to get to know people before judging them. If you keep an open mind, you can change the way you feel based on new information. Remember, prejudice and racism are based on ignorance.

Ari and his friends decided to go to the movies. It was Saturday afternoon, and a really hot new movie had just opened. After calling all of his friends to make plans,

Fashion magazines show a very limited range of beauty.

The amount of exposure you have to people of different races depends greatly on where you live.

they decided to meet up outside the theater about ten minutes beforehand to get tickets and popcorn.

When they all met up at the theater, they got a little noisy. They noticed some of the people on line were giving them dirty looks. One guy said, "Why don't you pull up your pants, you bum." Ari was used to getting comments like that, but he couldn't understand why people always assumed he and his friends were troublemakers. They weren't doing anything wrong. He wanted to say something back to the guy, but he decided just to ignore him.

Can you relate to Ari's story? Here are some other teens sharing their feelings about being stereotyped or judged for their race or the way they look. You too may have had experiences like these.

"When you walk into a store you get used to being followed. Sometimes I feel uncomfortable when I'm not being followed. You get used to white ladies reaching for their purses on the train. Everything becomes natural for you."
    —Jose, Dominican, 15 years old

"I did get stereotyped in my country. The people said that Bosnians were not civilized as much as other Yugoslavian people. But they are wrong. I think that all people deserve a chance to prove themselves. I wouldn't want someone to do it to me. I hate it when people make racist jokes. It's awful."
    —anonymous, Bosnian, 17 years old

"I've been prejudiced. I can recall times when I've heard a white boy my age listening to 'black' music and wearing 'black' clothes, and I caught myself thinking that he was trying to be black. Mostly I feel stereotyped by white people who have thought that because I have dark skin that I'm going to steal something, misbehave, or talk loud."
    —Felicity, biracial (black/white), 15 years old

"I heard on the news that the Better Business Bureau of Manhattan sent out a letter to stores on Fifth Avenue

[where the Puerto Rican Day Parade takes place] *telling them to close down on the day of the parade because Puerto Ricans might steal from their stores. I get stereotyped by everyone. They probably can't assume that I will grow up to be somebody."*
   —Amma, African American/West Indian, 15 years old

"I've experienced racism in school from students who would look down on me or doubt my ability because of my race and financial status."
   —anonymous, West Indian, 18 years old

"Since early in childhood in school and everywhere, people stare, make comments, or harass me about my eyes (I'm Korean) and the way I talk. I've been stereotyped as a nerd and called Chinese."
   —Jennifer, Korean, 17 years old

   When these kinds of situations happen, you may feel a lot of different emotions. So what can you do when you have experiences like the ones above? Is there any way to avoid being stereotyped by someone else or prejudging others before you know them? To find out how to cope with and fight against racial prejudice, keep reading.

Chapter 4

How to Cope with Racism

This chapter is a very important part of the book. In it you will find the practical advice of professionals and other teens, like you, who have experienced racism and prejudice in many different situations.

Mina is fourteen years old. She started high school this year. She is one of the few students of color at her new private school. Mina had attended public school for her whole life, but her parents wanted her to have the opportunity to experience a different school environment. Now she feels a little out of place and different. Most of her new classmates already know each other from their private junior high schools. Almost everyone lives in the area surrounding the school, which is a wealthy white neighborhood. Mina has to take an hour-and-a-half bus ride to school every morning from her working-class black neighborhood. At lunchtime she eats alone. The pretty and popular girls are the ones who are skinny and blond, and they hang out with all the cute jocks. Being one of the only black students in her classes makes Mina uncomfortable. The worst is when they discuss slavery in history class. It seems like everyone thinks she knows everything there is to know about black people and black history. Mina sometimes wishes that she wasn't so obviously different from her classmates.

But it bothers her even more when her teachers won't call on her at all. She's beginning to think her teachers assume that because she is black she won't know the answer. Mina has no idea whom to talk to about this. She's thinking of asking her parents to let her transfer to another school closer to home. When she is in her neighborhood she fits right in, but here she feels very negative about herself.

Racism has had such a powerful effect that sometimes those who have suffered from it may try different ways of avoiding it or dealing with it. Some people try to ignore it, some try harder to fit in. Others may try to lose their accent, wear the "right" clothes, change their hair, wear contact lenses, or deny that they like a certain kind of food or music. In other words, some people may try to deny their heritage in an attempt to be accepted. It's easy to see why some people feel they need to change themselves instead of just being themselves. Unfortunately, these ideas about fitting in and being like

Teachers can offer support and advice if you are feeling discouraged about the racism you see or experience.

everybody else are reinforced by many different people in our society.

In Mina's case, it was her teachers who were reinforcing these negative ideas. Being one of the few students of color at her school made her feel as if something was wrong with her. Some of her teachers treated her differently than her classmates. When a person says or does something racist to you, it can feel like a slap in the face. If it happens over and over, you might start to believe what you are being told.

If you are continually in situations where you feel that people have low expectations of you, then you too may begin to have low expectations for yourself and end up not caring at all. This can be the case if you

41

don't already have a strong set of expectations for yourself. For example, if your teacher assumes you don't know the answer and never calls on you, then you may end up making no effort and not participating in class. You think your teacher doesn't care, so why should you?

These negative feelings about your abilities can lead to anger, sadness, discouragement, or even overcompensation—trying desperately to fit in and prove the racist is wrong. These are very real and serious emotions that must be addressed. You may begin to feel hopeless when you realize that no matter what you do, or how hard you work, others see only a negative stereotype of you. They do not see the individual. It can be hard to accept that some people will never change the way they think about you.

A Teacher's Advice

How can Mina cope with the racism she experiences in the classroom? Cassius Gil, a high school teacher in New York, has some suggestions. "When a student comes to me with a complaint about a teacher being prejudiced, I ask questions first to make sure the teacher really is being racist and not just strict. Then, if I decide the student is right, I tell [him or her] that the only thing [he or she] can do is work twice as hard, so the teacher has to give a good grade."

Gil also suggests that students keep all of their class notes, test scores, and papers, so that if a teacher should grade them unfairly, they will be able to show proof of their work. Gil also says it's important to talk to other teachers who care about you or to the principal, so that they know what's going on before it becomes a problem. This way they have a record of complaints. If the situation persists, file a complaint with the school board.

There are ways for you to cope with the effects of racism without letting it destroy your faith in people or your self-confidence. One psychologist advises that you pick your battles. This is important because it is impossible to respond to everything all the time. You have only so much energy. If you tried to fight every racist battle you encountered, you might be frustrated and angry a lot of the time. In some situations it is important to speak up, but there are also other effective ways of dealing with racism that focus on making yourself stronger and more knowledgeable.

Know Your History

The best way to put things in perspective is to learn about your history. There are many books that can give you an understanding into what your community has gone through in order to survive (see For Further Reading at the end of this book). Learn why certain traditions are practiced and in what ways history keeps repeating itself. Knowing this type of information can help you if you ever decide to confront someone's bigoted remarks. Remember, often a person's prejudice is based on lack of knowledge.

Responding to a racist remark isn't easy, but you may feel
good about taking a stand.

Learn from Your Elders

Many of us come from communities that believe in
respecting and cherishing our elders and our ancestors
because they have lived through a lot. They can share
a great deal of wisdom. Ask them about when they
were children and about their lives. Hearing their stories may help you to see your family's successes and
accomplishments.

Have Cultural Heroes

Think about how often you look to television and the
movies for your role models. While there are positive
celebrity role models, look around your community as
well. There are sure to be people you admire for their

courage or their commitment to something you find important. You can find out about people of color in your community who are doing extraordinary things. Learn from them how they cope with the pressures and still manage to be successful.

Find a Mentor

This is especially important for those of you who are in the minority at school or in your neighborhood. Sometimes it may seem that you are the only person going through a hard time. But there are older people who can be a great help when you are going through tough times. Talking to someone who is outside of your peer group is a good way to feel supported. Many schools, churches, and colleges have mentoring programs.

Understand That Race Isn't Always the Issue

Sometimes when you are Asian, Latino, Native American, or African American, you may think that the only thing people notice about you is your race. Sometimes this is true, but not always. You would do yourself a disservice if you assumed that every time something bad happened to you it was because the other person was a racist. You might miss out on some valuable friendships. If you are always expecting racist treatment from other people, you may be creating problems where there aren't any.

Say Something

If someone makes a racist remark to you, you may decide it's best not to say anything. It can depend on your situation. But sometimes you may decide it's worth it to say something. It takes courage to speak your mind, but it can make you feel good to take a stand for something you believe in, whether or not the comment is directed at you. Here are some things you might try saying. A note of caution, however. If the person you are addressing is aggressive or angry, you should walk away and report the confrontation to an authority—especially if you're physically threatened.

> *"What you said was rude and disrespectful."*
> *"I think you should apologize for saying that."*

If the remark wasn't directed at you, you can still respond with the above statements, but you might add:

> *"I don't think those kinds of comments are funny."*
> *"I think you should apologize to my friend."*

Or you can always walk away.

Talk About It

It is always a good idea to talk about your feelings about racism. The most comfortable setting for this is often among people who have been through the same thing—otherwise you may find yourself teaching rather than sharing. Some high school and college campuses have cultural groups and classes that address issues of racism.

File a Report

You may decide to report an act of racism. If you are physically threatened or hurt, or if you feel you are being discriminated against on the job or at school, you may decide to take action. Speak to your parents about it first. They may be able to help you decide on a proper course of action. Speak to a community leader who may be able to offer support.

The first thing to do is write down what happened. Try to be as objective as you can when reporting the event. Use words that honestly describe the act. Write down where it happened and when it happened. Be as clear as possible. This will help your case if and when you go to court. Remember, filing a complaint isn't easy. But if you feel strongly about what happened to you or someone else, take action.

Chapter 5

Making a Difference

"I wish I didn't have to go and work at a soup kitchen today," thought Andy. He would much rather spend the afternoon rollerblading around the neighborhood with his friends. But as part of his school requirements, he must perform community service. There was no choice but to go.

He was a little worried because the soup kitchen was in a part of the city that he didn't know very well. When his parents drove through that part of town, they usually checked to make sure the car doors were locked. The area was pretty poor and run down, and there were a lot of homeless people and minorities there. "I might get mugged," thought Andy, whose own neighborhood was a quiet, suburban area. Andy didn't really feel like dealing with all of this today. He just wanted to chill out with his friends and have fun.

When Andy arrived at the soup kitchen for his shift, he was shocked to see how many people were waiting to eat. He was even more surprised that they weren't the kind of people he had expected to see. There were people of all races, and, most surprisingly, there were a lot of women with children. "On TV the people who go to soup kitchens are always poor black guys," thought Andy. "But here there are many white people and women and children."

In this final chapter we will try to address the question of how you can stop the hate and prejudice you see around you. It starts with yourself. It would be wonderful if we could simply wish away racism and prejudice. But life isn't that simple, and we all have a darker side that stereotypes people and judges them for the color of their skin. Overcoming our own prejudice is a part of our lives, whether we like it or not. But we can deal with that by being aware of our prejudices and working to avoid them. As we have seen in this book, racism comes wrapped in some very difficult issues.

For example, according to the law, cabdrivers should not discriminate against their passengers. But in many cities in the United States, cabdrivers refuse to pick up passengers because of their race. Some cabdrivers believe it is their right to refuse, saying that there is a higher possibility they will be robbed or physically threatened by certain passengers. But what about the person who can't get a cab home at midnight no matter how many times he or she tries? The former mayor of New York City, David Dinkins (who is a black man), on one occasion could not get a cab to stop for him—even as the Mayor of New York City! We must tell cabdrivers and all people who work in jobs that serve the people that they must perform their jobs. They cannot discriminate against people based on race.

Do Unto Others...

Once we have realized our own prejudices, we can try to build common bonds with people of all races. It's impossible to walk in another person's shoes (experience their life as they do), but that doesn't mean we should stop trying to understand each other. It's important to learn to empathize. That means trying to identify with other people. We also try to understand and be sensitive to their thoughts, experiences, and feelings.

When we experience prejudice directed at ourselves we know it is unfair. It is also unfair when we do it to others. One of the most important steps in stopping racism is realizing that it is just as harmful when we are prejudiced toward others. The best way to bridge the distances and differences between "us" and "them" is to get to know each other. Sit down and talk. Instead of stereotyping individuals based on a whole group, get to know the person.

Andy made that mistake when he went to the soup kitchen. He stereotyped the people whom he would be

As you learn more about a person, you'll likely find that you have more in common than you thought.

serving before he even met them. Change begins with one-to-one relationships. Once you get to know people who are different, you may still dislike some of them, but it will be for individual traits, not because of the color of their skin or the clothes they wear. Once you get to know an individual and learn about what makes him or her unique, then you can find things in common. When you treat all people with respect, others will treat you in the same manner. But when you treat others with hatred and fear, then they may do the same to you.

Sometimes it may seem that racism and prejudice will never be completely erased from our society. Many of you have probably felt as if there were nothing you could do. You may not be able to enlighten people who don't want to change their racist attitudes. But you do have power and you can change your own attitudes. And that is how you begin to make a difference in our society.

We suggested some ways of coping with racism in the last chapter. Those suggestions were meant as advice on how to keep racism and prejudice from hurting. Following are some important steps to take toward changing your own attitudes and the attitudes of others about racism and prejudice.

"If you are neutral in situations of injustice, you have chosen the side of the oppressor."

—Desmond Tutu, Archbishop Emeritus of South Africa

Confront

When it's appropriate and when you feel safe and comfortable doing so, confront the forms of hatred, racism, and prejudice that you encounter. This means addressing racism in your family, with friends, coworkers, and yourself. Monitor your own thoughts and feelings. When you think negatively of another person or group of people, ask yourself what those thoughts are based on. Are your thoughts based on feelings or facts? No racial slurs should be acceptable. Language is a powerful tool of hatred. Think about how horrible some racial slurs sound—then think about how much worse it must feel to be called those words.

If you feel comfortable, confront racism even if it comes from a friend and is not directed at you.

Recognize Similarities

We are all individuals, and inevitably we have differences. But remember that we also share many traits and feelings. For example, no one wants to be rejected by others. We are all hurt by prejudice and racism. Ultimately, everyone wants to be understood. These are common bonds that can connect people of all races.

Accept

Taking pride in your own heritage does not make you a racist. It's also important, however, to accept people's differences. You can appreciate who you are and still have room to appreciate other kinds of people. This is not an easy thing to do. Even when you try to accept

As the country becomes more diverse, your circle of friends may grow more diverse as well.

other people, you may clash in your ideas and opinions. It's impossible to like everyone we meet, but we should all try to be more tolerant of other cultures and lifestyles. This country is becoming more and more diversified. It's in everyone's best interest to accept others. Diversity is a positive thing, and one you can learn from.

Volunteer

Make an effort to volunteer and perform community service. Volunteering helps to bridge racial and cultural divisions. It can expose you to people with different life experiences from your own. It will also make you feel good to be contributing to the community. You can find places to volunteer through public listings in your local newspaper, at the public library's bulletin board, and through your place of worship. You may want to check your high school's counseling department. You may also want to work with children to help them learn about these issues.

Keep an Open Mind

Try to have an open mind about all people and experiences. Try to see people for who they are, not how they look. You must make an effort. We are all comfortable with what we are used to, but if you want to broaden your horizons it's important to get out of your comfort zone and meet different people. Consider joining a group that promotes interaction among people of different races. There may be a group in your community that already does this. If not, start your own group. Then when you do get together with a person of another race, look for things that you have in common. Focus on the similarities, not the differences.

Take a Stand in the Fight Against Racism

While you are trying to change your own ideas and those in your community, you can extend the fight against racism even further. Remember how much the media can foster stereotypes? Pay attention to what you watch on television and what you read in the newspapers. If you don't like something you see or read, write a letter. The media and their advertisers consider you valuable consumers. They will listen to what you have to say. Let them know when they are contributing to racist attitudes and stereotypes. And remember, you don't have to experience racism yourself to fight against it.

These may seem like small efforts, but every effort is a step in the right direction.

Glossary

abolitionist In the 1800s, a person who fought to end slavery.

assassinate To murder by sudden or secret attack, usually for personal or political reasons.

bigotry Acts and beliefs of a person who strongly holds on to his or her intolerance and prejudice.

boycott To refuse to deal with a person, store, or organization as a way to express disapproval or force them to accept certain conditions.

discrimination To treat someone differently for reasons other than individual merit, such as race, gender, class, or religion.

diverse Having different elements; varied.

empathize To understand and be sensitive to another's thoughts and feelings without actually having those thoughts or feelings.

enlighten To give knowledge or to instruct.

heritage Culture and traditions that are handed down from previous generations.

ignorance Lack of knowledge.

immigration Entry into another country to live.

intimidate To influence by fear.

persecution Mistreatment of a person because of his or her beliefs.

prejudice Judgment or opinion of someone or something without adequate knowledge.

segregation The separation of people of different races in schools, restaurants, hospitals, and other such places.

stereotype An oversimplified opinion of a group of people based on general or limited information.

unconstitutional Not allowed by the Constitution of the United States.

white supremacy The belief that white people are superior to all other races.

Where to Go for Help

American Civil Liberties Union (ACLU)
The national ACLU cannot process requests for assistance but suggests you check your local phone book for the number of the office near you.
Web site: http://www.aclu.org

Anti-Defamation League
823 United Nations Plaza
New York, NY 10017
(212) 490-2525
Web site: http://www.adl.org

The CityKids Foundation
57 Leonard Street
New York, NY 10013
(212) 925-3320
Web site: http://www.citykids.com
This organization gives workshops and performances across the country to promote racial harmony.

Community Cousins
c/o Diane Birnie Bock
140 Encinitas Boulevard, Suite 220
Encinitas, CA 92024
(760) 944-CUZZ (2899)
e-mail: dnabrd@aol.com
This nonprofit group matches individuals and families of different backgrounds. They can help you start a group in your community. Call for a free manual.

Council for Unity, Inc.
50 Avenue X
Brooklyn, NY 11223
attn: Carlos Menendez
Web site:: http://www.councilforunity.org
This organization gives advice and information on what you
can do to improve racial relations at your school.

HateWatch
HateWatch monitors hate-group activity on the Internet.
Groups are listed by category and country.
Web site: http://www.hatewatch.org

National Association for the Advancement of
   ## Colored People (NAACP)
To find a local chapter, look in your telephone book under
listings for associations.
Web site: http://www.naacp.org

In Canada:

Artists Against Racism
Box 54511
Toronto, Ontario M5M 4N5
(416) 410-5631
Web site: http://aar.vrx.net
email: aar@idirect.com
This nonprofit international organization uses many youth
idols, such as musicians, actors, and writers, to help teens
combat racial and religious prejudice.

For Further Reading

Chideya, Farai. *Don't Believe the Hype*. New York:
    Plume Books, 1995.
Cockcoft, James D. *The Hispanic Struggle for Social
    Justice: The Hispanic Experience in the Americas*.
    New York: Franklin Watts, 1994.
Garza, Hedda and Rober Green. *African Americans
    and Jewish Americans: A History of Struggle*.
    New York: Franklin Watts, 1996.
Griffin, Howard. *Black Like Me*. New York: Signet,
    1961.
Haley, Alex. *Autobiography of Malcolm X*. New York:
    Ballantine Books, 1964.
Katz, William. *The Westward Movement and
    Abolitionism, 1815-1860 (A History of
    Multicultural America)*. Milwaukee, WI:
    Raintree/Steck Vaughn, 1992.
Levine, Ellen. *Freedom's Children: Young Civil Rights
    Activists Tell Their Own Stories*. New York:
    Avon, 1995.
Manetti, Lisa. *Equality*. New York: Franklin Watts,
    1989.

Morrison, Toni. *The Bluest Eye*. New York: Washington Square Press, 1970.

Movas, Himilce. *Everything You Need to Know About Latino History.* New York: Plume Books, 1994.

Muse, Daphne. *Prejudice: Stories About Hate, Ignorance, Revelation, and Transformation.* New York: Hyperion, 1995.

Osborn, Kevin. *Tolerance*. New York: The Rosen Publishing Group, 1993.

Wirths, Claudine, and Mary Bowman-Kruhm. *Coping with Discrimination and Prejudice.* New York: The Rosen Publishing Group, 1998.

Index

About the Author
Nasoan Sheftel-Gomes is a freelance writer living in New York City. She has
a BA from Clark University in Sociology and Women's Studies and a
Masters of Journalism from the University of California at Berkeley.
Nasoan grew up in San Francisco, the child of a Jewish-American mother
and an African-American/Cape-Verdean father.

Photo Credits
Photo on p.7 by Reuters/Sam Mircovich/Archive Photos: pp..10, 14, 18 by
Photoworld/ FPG International; p.13 by Archive Photos; p.16 by Express
Newspapers/H392?Archive Photos; p.22 by AP/Wide World Photos; p.25 by
FPG International; cover and all other photos by Ira Fox.